Where I Eat My Bread...
Stories of in-migration to the Highlands & Islands

**"Well, my heart's in the Highlands,
I'm gonna go there
when I feel good enough to go."**

Bob Dylan – *"Highlands"*
after Robert Burns'
"My Heart's in the Highlands"

Cha d`dhuin doras nach d`fhosgail doras

Gaelic Proverb
"No door ever closed but another opened."

First published in Great Britain in 2016 by Robert Brian
MacLeod
259 Tubeg, Skerray, by Thurso KW14 7TJ

ISBN 978-1-910205-81-5

Printed and bound by For The Right Reasons,
60 Grant St Inverness. IV3 8BS
fortherightreasons@rocketmail.com
01463 718844 or 07717 457 247

Price: £8.50

THE
STRATHMARTINE
TRUST

Many thanks
to the
Strathmartine
Trust for
their support
and funding
towards this
project.

Contents...

Foreword by Dr James Hunter...

Brian MacLeod lives in Tubeg, one of the several townships constituting the crofting district of Skerray on Sutherland's north coast. To get there from the south is to travel through the most comprehensively depopulated landscapes in Britain.

During the Highland Clearances, Sutherland's landlords emptied the county's interior to make way for sheep farms. In more recent times, coastal localities like Skerray – their tiny crofts a product of a nineteenth-century need to find dumping places for folk evicted from inland localities – have themselves seen family after family leave in search of better prospects. Sutherland, as a result, is one of the few extensive areas – whether in Britain or Europe more generally – where there are today far fewer people than there were 200 years ago.

From the rising ground immediately behind the croft house he shares with his wife Irene, Brian gestures towards buildings that have fallen into disuse, fields that are no longer cultivated. "Day after day," he says, "radio and television news reports are given over to what's called a 'migrant crisis'. Day after day we're told the UK's full up, overcrowded. Well, that certainly isn't true of this part of the country. Here we're crying out for people."

What's encouraging in this context is that, despite a continuing drift away from Sutherland's north coast, the Highlands and Islands as a whole have of late been making progress in stemming an exodus that, from the 1840s until the 1960s, led to the region's population falling decade by decade. This matters hugely. It's hard to have faith in the future of a place where it has become received wisdom – as was the case in much of the Highlands and Islands for much of the twentieth century – that, should you wish to get on in the world, you'd better start by getting out. Hence the significance of the fact that, over the last 30 or 40 years, many more people have been moving into the Highlands than have been going away.

Who are those people? Why are they here? What do they do and what do they think of the places where they've chosen to settle? Surprisingly little effort has been made to answer these questions.

Many commentators on the Highlands and Islands, myself included, have written a great deal about the folk who left our area in the past. But few such commentators, myself again included, have explored the antecedents, motivations and experiences of our immigrants. That's why this publication is important. It tells us a lot about people who, by making their homes here, have changed and are changing the Highlands and Islands greatly for the better.

Brian MacLeod has had a long involvement in community development in the Highlands and Islands. Mostly he worked in rural areas such as Shetland and Skye. In 2003, however, he became community project officer in Merkinch – a part of Inverness. It was there, Brian comments, he became aware for the first time of the sheer diversity of Highland Scotland's newer residents.

"I'd always thought of Inverness as a wee town where everybody shared much the same sort of background," he says. "Then I discovered that there were getting on for 50 different languages spoken by children attending Inverness schools. Inverness, I realised, was becoming more and more cosmopolitan. And what's true of Inverness, I discovered, is true – even if not to quite the same extent – of other Highlands and Islands communities. That's illustrated, I think, by the stories I've collected."

Brian takes care to stress there was nothing systematic about his selection of interviewees. They're simply people he's come across or been put in touch with – one interviewee, in some instances, suggesting others. His model, he explains, is the work of the late Studs Terkel – easily the most renowned of America's oral historians.

Brian produces a battered and faded copy of Terkel's 1974 classic, *Working* – subtitled *People Talk About What They Do All Day and How They Feel About What They Do*. He bought this book, Brian says, when, as a Stirling University student, he got the chance to spend a semester in California.

He points to an introductory paragraph where Terkel reflects on what can be learned from first recording an interview and then, while still in the interviewee's presence, listening to what has been recorded. "On one occasion during a play-back," Terkel wrote, "my companion murmured in wonder, 'I never realised I felt that way.'

"And I was filled with wonder too."

He's had much the same sort of experience, Brian comments. He instances his interview with Petra and Arafeh Alashi – and in particular Arafeh's recollection of how, not long after he'd moved into Tong, a crofting village on the Isle of Lewis, a neighbour provided him with what Arafeh, during his interview, calls a "lovely casserole". "Oh I enjoyed it!" Arafeh remembers. "This was hospitality ... it said to me, you are welcome."

"It's encouraging to hear that sort of thing," Brian says. "In so much of the media coverage of our response to migrants and to refugees the emphasis is all the time on problems, tensions, hostility. But talk with folk who have moved into the Highlands and Islands – often from very far away – and you're told, over and over again, that this is a good place to come to, a place where people, whatever their origins, are made to feel at home.

"That's not to say that Highlanders and Islanders are more accepting of newcomers than anyone else. It's more to do with the fact that once individual immigrants, or immigrant families, get the chance to get established somewhere, then people can see them for what they are – not some sort of invading mass but folk who, you begin to realise, aren't all that different from everyone else."

Which brings Brian MacLeod back to his starting point. "Think of all the Sutherland communities that were destroyed in the course of the clearances," he comments. "Think of all the land that's been unpopulated ever since. Think of the way that so many of our people got the chance to make new lives for themselves in countries such as the US or Canada or Australia. Wouldn't it be good if, by one means or another, we could find a way of having some part at least of Sutherland reoccupied by families who are fleeing – just like our own folk once had to do – from danger and oppression?"

That, perhaps, is a project for another day. For the moment it's a big step forward to have access to the voices of immigrants who are already with us in the Highlands and Islands – immigrants whom you'll meet and get to know a little when you read the words Brian's taken so much trouble to record, transcribe and now get into print.

James Hunter

Introduction...

These short stories are first-hand accounts by people who are part of the continuing and constant flow of humanity into new lands across borders and cultures. They might be referred to as incomers – but then we are all incomers, and we are all migrants – if you go back far enough.

We might call them New Highlanders and that description allows them to be part of this mix of people who over many years have settled in the North of Scotland.

George Mackay Brown referred to the many folk who migrated to Orkney during the late '60s and '70s as the "*Greening of Orkney*". They brought new ideas and new energy to keep the public halls going and to turn over the soil.

These accounts of individual lives give us an insight into the difficulties and challenges of moving into a new land and culture. But they are much more than that – the contributors' honesty and humour as they reflect on their own and their families' experiences allow us to begin to understand and empathise with their journey – physical and cultural. In a small way they can throw light on the various ways in which our life in the Highlands and Islands is being strengthened by the wide variety of experiences and talents that new folk bring.

We know that so many from Scotland have emigrated over the years to other lands and we know how they played their part in developing other countries. Maybe those migrants had the same energy, courage and open-ness to new ways that these stories illustrate.

This wee book is dedicated to the heroes featured herein. They warmly welcomed me and generously told their stories. I learned so much about our common shared humanity. For me it has been a real pleasure and a privilege to hear these stories first hand.

I hope you enjoy reading of their adventures.

Robert Brian MacLeod
Sgeireadh
Duthaich MhicAoidh

Elsie Cardosi – Wick

My grandfather left Italy and came over here in 1892. He went to Shetland right away because he had an older sister living in Shetland and in those days you needed a sponsor.

He was working in the fishing and he stayed there until 1906. He had been saving a bit of money so he bought the Fisherman's Saloon at the harbour here in Wick, now operating as "Wickers World". He did well there; I can mind my father telling me how grandfather made £30 in one morning. My Granny used to stack the gold sovereigns in piles of ten. He ran it as a café but he was one of the first to make ice-cream. Later the family had three cafes in Wick. The café in Thurso was started by my grandfather's brother much later and he made his money once Dounreay arrived.

In 1910 he married an Italian and brought her over here and they had three sons, but through time the three sons went back to Italy and married Italian girls and brought them over here.

My parents got married in 1933 and that is when my mother arrived in Scotland. My two sisters and I were all born here. I was born in Wick in 1947.

When my mother travelled from Italy the train broke down two miles out of Wick and she thought she was on another planet! She had to walk in the last two miles and they had been three days travelling by train – you can imagine how she felt. This was in November – she thought she was at the end of the world, she really did. I think, you know, she was quite unhappy really when she first came over here in 1933.

She stayed down at the harbour and was living with her in-laws and she was looking after Grand-dad and Granny and my two uncles and her husband and she had a little lassie then. Hard, very hard times. She was 14 years down at the harbour but then they got a house with the café here in the High St and when she moved there it was a little better, at least she had a place of her own – but she had a hard life.

One of the hardest events to endure for all Italian immigrants and even those born in Scotland was Internment. German nationals were held separately as prisoners of war.

My mother and father were forcibly separated as my father was interned in the Isle of Man during the war. In June 1941 they came: the police at 4 o`clock in the morning and they  nearly put the door in. The police knew my father, they knew him very well but they frightened the wits out of everybody. They took him away – although he was lucky in that he missed going on that ship the *Arandora Star* which was torpedoed in 1940.

He was held there on the Isle of Man for four years with many other Italians. He worked on a farm there – Kelly`s farm. He and others who worked in the countryside might come back to camp with a rabbit or a chicken and maybe pick some wild herbs and there were, you know, plenty chefs amongst the internees, so they could cook up something a bit Italian!

They went off in the morning and did not come back till six at night but my father said Farmer Kelly was ever so good to them.

My mother, as the wife of an alien was not allowed to remain in Wick because all the land north of Inverness was designated a "protected area".

She had to stay in Glasgow in lodgings with her sister but she crossed the Irish sea seven times to visit my father during his internment.

(Elsie treasures a beautiful model of a fishing smack carved and crafted by one of her father's fellow internees, Salvatori Lauro - he is related to the Laoro family shipping line from Naples).

I can remember my father telling me that during the war here some people would be throwing bricks at the windows of the shop because of Mussolini joining forces with Hitler even although the Italians had fought alongside the British in the First World War. There was a lot of bitterness.

My older sister had gone to Italy for a holiday with her Granny and Grand-dad in 1939, but of course the war broke out and she never got back till she was fourteen. My whole family was split up as a result of the war and my older sister and I, we don't really know each other that well.

After the war they came back and picked up the businesses and kept going – although rationing meant that sugar was scarce and no ice-cream could be made. But my father had to work on a farm; a government requirement as internees were "on Parole". Seven times my father asked to receive British Nationality and seven times he was rejected – he never asked again. "Collar the lot". That is what Winston Churchill declared.

My sister came back from Italy after the war with very little English and was very bitter about being separated from her family for so long. It disrupted every family.

I have never felt the need to move to Italy but these days given that Ian my husband and I are retired we can go back for months at a time. But you know when I am in Italy I am not Italian and when I am in Scotland I am not Scottish. It is how you were brought up with Scottish ways or Italian ways. You don't know where you are – where is home? Wherever I am staying!

They are very family-orientated over there in Italy – you still have "children" living at home until they are married and that might be at age thirty or older.

My parents of course were second generation: my father was born here, he went to school here, but it must have been difficult for my grandfather coming straight from Italy. It was difficult for my mother – not speaking the language.

I worked in the shop until my father died but then we sold the business and I worked in Riverside nursing home and the laundry at the harbour until I retired. Looking back it has been completely different, the life in Italy and in Scotland. The way children are brought up; the bairns in Italy don't go to bed until about midnight, but they are maybe a bit over-protected as part of this wide family.

But the older folk are always looked after by the family as well – they don't go into nursing homes. In the country areas in particular the expectation is that the children will look after their parents in their own home. But here the young ones often move away and there is no family to look after the older ones.

Richard Cardosi – Thurso

My grandfather left Italy for Glasgow in 1903 at the age of 18. He already had three older brothers in Glasgow.

They had all been born in the Barga district of Italy, but the Cardosi family had been active there in the building trade and they had a small farm with a vineyard. So they were well enough set up – they didn't come over here with nothing.

A lot of Barga folk came over to Scotland, settling particularly in Glasgow. I think you could say that the majority of Italians who migrated to the South of Scotland originated in Barga. In fact these days there is even an annual fish and chip festival held in Barga.

After working for a while with his brothers in Glasgow and Paisley my grandfather, Joseph Cardosi headed north to join his oldest brother Peter who had shops in Wick and Thurso, so my grandfather came up to work for him. He started work in Thurso and eventually he took over the shop in Thurso. In Wick the family had three shops – that was the Cardosis, but we were also related to the Cabrellis who also had businesses.

When they arrived in Scotland they generally fitted into the community.

Why did they get into fish and chips and ice-cream? I have no idea.

My grandfather (Nonno) went back to Italy every other year – he travelled back and forth. Not immediately after the war because no one could travel anywhere. I went to University in 1953 and my mother and father went over to Italy for their first visit about then.

My Nonno was the youngest of the brothers; he was working in the cafés.

When I was four years old there was a fish and chip shop in Swanson Street, now Brasses shop. My Nonno owned practically the whole of that square.

He also owned a couple of houses up town – but just before the war he took tenancy of the Central Hotel. My father bought the Central and surrounding property in the mid-50s.

Internment:

Peter Pieraccini had the wireless shop and he was interned

alongside Bertie (Alberto) Cardosi who was Elsie`s father. They were very abrupt in picking them up, but when you look back on it, there was a war on and there were bound to be some repercussions.

My Nonno took British citizenship before 1910 and served in the Royal Artillery during World War I. My father was in the Royal Air Force during World War II.

My grandfather never suffered any personal attacks because the old ones of the fishing community remembered when they had had hard times he had been a benefactor. And of course the fisherman reciprocated any favours – when he came down in the morning there might be a parcel of fish at the back door.

I always said there were two great men in my life: Winston Churchill and Joseph Cardosi – but not necessarily in that order! I thought the world of him. He was a very generous man. He managed to keep going through the war years and after.

I worked at Dounreay for over two years, 1957/58. Then my father had just bought property and my brother had got out of the army early and he wanted to come home – by this time I was working in the shop.

My father said to us, look, we will start a restaurant upstairs. So he says to me, "Can you run a restaurant?" – I said, "I'll give it a try." So we opened the restaurant in 1961 and Raymond, my brother, went into the shop.

I was offered a partnership in the restaurant – a third I think it was – and that went on until after the mid-60s. And then as flats became vacant we did them up and I thought right, we could convert this property into a hotel. And that is what we did: 10 bedrooms, bar and restaurant.

We were as a family very well accepted up here, but my father was born here and he married a local girl so we are related to local folk. I am tremendously proud of my Italian heritage and I am proud of my family connections on both sides.

Heinz Voigt, Unwilling Immigrant! – Germany

I was born in 1925 in the Saxony District of Germany – near Dresden; like many I was a member of the Hitler Youth Movement. I was only 14 at the start of the war and I started an apprenticeship in accountancy – but the war came along.

My apprenticeship was shortened and we were drafted into technical support for the army. I spent six months digging ditches and then received army training in Leipzig. I was then transferred into the army and stationed in France, near Brest. We later saw combat in Brittany.

One morning the bombardment started and I saw an American Tank approaching – so we hid behind a farmhouse high up in a pile of brushwood. We thought that once the tank passed by we could make it back to our own lines.

But suddenly there was a tremendous explosion above me and I couldn`t see a thing. It must have been one of the Americans who threw a hand grenade up and it exploded above me. I had shrapnel all over the place, my neck and arms and there is still one in there (*points to foot*). I was wounded and bleeding with a head wound as the shrapnel had pierced my helmet.

So that was that – I was captured by the Americans. They bandaged me up and eventually at a field hospital they picked out all these bits and pieces of shrapnel.

We were taken to the coast and across to Britain as our captors weren`t quite sure what Hitler was going to do.

When I think about it now – I was lucky to be captured by the Yanks –best of equipment and no shortage of food or nothing! So we were taken up to Glasgow and into a troop ship and across the Atlantic, I arrived in New York. In this centre we were told "throw all your clothes and uniform away – you will get everything new." It was I suppose to de-contaminate us. We wore American uniforms – but dyed black with POW on the back.

So then on to a train in a crowded compartment and for five days we travelled across country to Arizona. This was in June and it was bloody steaming hot over there; mind you, the American barracks seemed like luxury, white buildings with red roofs and all facilities showers and everything.

Absolutely terrific how they look after their soldiers over there it's marvellous. In that heat we were having a shower every couple of hours or so. Eventually we moved from there to California, they never told us why

we were moving but we found out when we arrived it was to do agricultural work: picking cotton or picking peaches. We picked peaches for Del Monte near Salinas, California.

The cotton-picking was hard: you had to fill huge six feet long bags with a shoulder strap. Oh dear – you had a quota to meet – they weighed the bags and everybody had to pick so much, you see. Some refused to work. As the war was still on they could refuse the work. So they just picked enough to make a pillow and lay down.

And some filled a bag and after the weigh-in they managed to throw the bag still full to the other side of the trailer and then queue up to weigh again! Another way to cheat the Yanks was to pick the wild water melons that grew alongside the cotton rows and put them in the sack – oh what nonsense!

There must have been about two hundred of us working and there were regular counts to see that we were all still present.

When the war ended Britain said to the US that the German POWs must return to Britain. So that's what happened; we were transported up to San Francisco and then into a big ship – under the Golden Gate and away south through the Panama Canal, a massive construction, and then back in to the Atlantic sailing by Cuba and on and on to Liverpool.

So they were telling us we would be going home, the war is finished so you can go home. We thought we would be released but, of course, what we did not know was that Britain had made this agreement with the US to transfer us to work again in the UK.

So I was unlucky enough to get back to Britain – but I am still here!

I was in a group that was put on a train up to Perth to the camp at Comrie, (POW transit camp) and then on to Dingwall. We were kept at Brahan Castle outside Dingwall.

A few of us were then put on the train to Golspie and then marched up the main street to Kirkton Farm where we were held again in Nissan huts. There were at least three Nissan huts there – I think the Italians were there before us.

I worked at Kirkton farm and a farm near Fearn where there was another camp. Three years after the war ended prisoners were being repatriated but I was from the area controlled by the Soviet Union and life was very poor there under Russian

occupation. I decided to stay on another year – I could delay the home-going but during that time I got involved with girlfriends and so...

There were quite a few of us that decided to stay on, one or two still alive. One of our number used to drive the lorry to take us to various farms; he is still alive but he has dementia now.

I worked with a farmer in Dornoch for quite a while and during that time a job came up with the *Northern Times* for a bookkeeper, so I applied for the job.

This was 1951 or 1952, anyway the editor was Bruce Weir at the time and he took a chance and engaged me – I stuck there for forty years!

We were treated OK I have no complaints, there were one or two farmers who were wary of us, but with some of them we were able to do a deal. The farmers were contracted to submit a time sheet to the Government and pay the agricultural wage to the Department of

Agriculture and then we received a few shillings direct from the Dept. But if they put half the hours down and then for the other hours they paid us direct – so they paid less and we got more.

I remember my mother and father were not very pleased when I wrote to say I was staying. It was 20 years later before I first travelled back to Germany. Since then I have gone back a few times – once we got a car it was easier. I have one sister left alive, and I will be 90 years old this year – in August.

When I was young and working for the *Northern Times* I used to go hillwalking, I have been all over the North and West Coast. A friend and I used to go every Sunday.

Looking back I must say that generally I was accepted as part of the North community although I was German. I think that working with the *Northern Times* helped.

I applied for British citizenship as I had established my life here; I could visit Germany and come back "home".

I think if new people could work like I did it might help them feel at home.

Suleiman Makhouli – Amman Jordan

I was born in Amman Jordan in 1950. I attended the British boarding school there – this is where our beloved King Hussein studied, I was there until 1967, and then I finished my schooling in Lebanon. My parents were in Kuwait where my father was working; they were planning to move to the Lebanon.

1967 was the year Israel took the East Jerusalem West Bank of Jordan and occupied parts of Syria and Egypt. They are still in occupation and the international community is saying do not build settlements in the West Bank and they are still building illegal settlements.

My family is from the Christian Anglican tradition in Jordan; there are a lot of Christians in Jordan, many people don't know this – I mean Jesus came from our country so we exported Christianity to you!

In the Lebanon, under the Constitution, the Head of State has to be of the Christian faith; this is still the case and again it is not widely known. I stayed in Lebanon for one year at the suggestion of an Anglican Minister who knew my father.

So after that year in Lebanon I came to Bath in England to study A-levels, I followed this with a computer programming course in London.

In the early 1970s my father was working in Kuwait with Kuwait Oil Company, so I went to join him in Kuwait. I worked in computers there, right through the '70s. It was whilst I was working there that I met my wife Maureen, from John o` Groats,

19

she was working as a midwife there. In 1979 we got married in Crawley, south of London where I had family. We went back to work in Kuwait and in 1980 the Iraq/Iran war began; the US was Saddam Husseion's friend. In 1987 it was a very dangerous time and there were rocket strikes near the shore of Kuwait not far from where Maureen and I worked. She wanted out. She left for Thurso and I carried on for a few more months, then I moved North.

We had visited Caithness over many years since we met, so I knew the place. When I first came I could not find a job here so I worked with British Airways in London. I worked as a translator and was in charge of meeting and greeting the VIPs arriving in Gatwick airport from all over the Arab world.

I remember I was buying a house in Crawley and I said to the estate agent I will get the money to you tomorrow and the next day Saddam Hussein invaded Kuwait! I had our savings in the bank in Kuwait and after the invasion you could not get your money out. This was on 2 August 1990 but my sister worked in the bank there and she was able to advise me and after some time I was able to transfer our money, but too late for the house.

It meant that Maureen and I accepted we should forget about the south and focus on living here in Thurso where we had rented a house next to the Salvation Army.

War has affected our lives but we are safe; when I look back to my time in Jordan the Israeli planes once flew over very low. That was frightening – but how the people in Syria are now living – it beggars belief, it is a crime. Any war, I don't care where it is, it is only benefiting the seller of arms. The only way to stop war is by talking, there is no other way.

I have seen war and... You know it is so sad, at Remembrance we say "Lest We Forget" and yet we go and bomb. We should sit and talk. Who is supplying the arms? Who is supplying them with money? These are the people that need to be stopped.

When I left my country I missed my family and extended family. I still have a sister who lives in Rafeedia and we still have a flat in Amman and a house in Beirut and we can go out and visit her there.

We have three children here: Philip born 1979, Jonathan born 1980, and Mark born 1982, all Highlanders born in the North but they are living away in Tunbridge Wells, Sydney and Fife!

I am a family man and I love it here – I go out for a dram now and again, I love my dram! The people are so friendly and I have so many good friends here. Over the years I coached football, the junior teams, and I still referee football games – even at my age – all over Caithness and Sutherland.

It was in 1992 that I opened the Sports shop in Thurso. We had darts champion Jocky Wilson along to open the shop, it was a great day there were crowds here. But business is difficult now with the internet.

It has helped being a Christian moving here, thank God. Going to church has helped me meet people. I think new people have to respect local traditions; they need to remember they are a guest here and act properly and responsibly.

You know the people up here are the nicest people I ever did meet, so friendly, now I have so many friends. I am one of them, I really do feel that.

You cannot have more welcoming people than up here and I think new arrivals will feel that. The landscape also, for me the sea helps when I think of the Mediterranean. I can feel at home here and the West it is so beautiful, when we have visitors we take them on a drive to see it.

Vaida Rasteborska – Lithuania

Born in Lithuania on the 19th July 1985 When I was finishing my second year of university in 2005, that summer two friends and myself decided we wanted to travel. As we had no money we needed to work and travel. In Vilnius we found a job and travel agency and we applied for the UK as we had been learning English at school.

We all got a job in Benbecula at the Dark Island Hotel. That was quite an experience. Wild landscape and few people but we were working a lot and we stayed with a lovely couple, Mr and Mrs McPhee, and we still keep in touch. On occasion we would go on a shopping spree to Inverness and we liked the town.

We returned to Lithuania to continue our studies and the next summer we came back, this time to Inverness. We stayed in the hostel in the High Street as it was cheaper and after a while we found jobs at Inverness Airport; we had good references from the Dark Island Hotel. It was catering work and it was a great experience because there were so many people from all over. We helped each other and we became friends. It was the place I met my future husband who is Polish.

Back to University and after that we wanted to be together, but he wasn`t keen on moving to Lithuania nor I to Poland so we came back to the place that we both knew – Inverness!

I am from a big family so of course I missed them and being able to see them every so often. Now my brothers and sister have children and we have two children so we try to get together every holiday we have. We are a close family and it seemed to me that families are not so close here in this country.

I had problems with the language at first so I went to college here in Inverness. But I still get confused – at home we use three languages English, Polish and Lithuanian. Although we are here in the Highlands we always think of our families in Poland and

Lithuania. My family have what you would call a croft and they have cattle, pigs and chickens – I miss all that. But we are settled here and we hope to stay for a while. I am studying Social Work through the Open University.

Thinking back we did hear people say things that were not very Customers at the airport might ask where you are from? And then you would hear them say, "Oh another Eastern European." This did make us feel uncomfortable, and we always are aware that there is this feeling that we are here taking local jobs. Well we had to remember that we are working hard and trying our best and of course we have to apply and go to interviews the same as everyone.

After a year I applied for a job with Highland Home Carers and in 2008 I started with them. My husband is kitchen manager in a local restaurant; it is a good job but hard work and long hours. Between us we can share the childcare but we don't see much of each other.

The last while has been hard because I was doing a practical placement through my social work studies and of course studying and sharing child care and with my husband working – for six months we did not have any day off together. But we are looking to the future... it will all be worthwhile – as I say we are settled here but it is difficult to say where home is: Poland? Lithuania? Scotland? I don't know, I have not applied for British citizenship; I feel somehow I might be betraying my own country. We are happy here and we hope our children can be brought up here and go to school here but after that who knows.

I would say to anyone who is thinking of moving to another country: think about what you are looking for, if you are motivated and a hard-working person then you can build a better life. You will have to take responsibility to create that life yourself.

I love Inverness it is not too big and I love the Highland landscape. I am very grateful for the opportunity I have been given at Highland Home Carers. Back home I took my degree in Social Pedagogy (Children and Families). Although it's not recognised in the UK and I had recently graduated, they had faith in me and gave me a job. For seven years I did home care and now I am going to work in the Leachkin Project. We have regular staff meetings and we all have an opportunity to raise ideas and concerns. As employees we are listened to and I really appreciate this.

Jurgita Skleinike – Lithuania

Born in Radviliskis, Lithuiania on 3rd April 1984. When I left school I went on to university and at that time I had no plans to move abroad. I made friends at University and after third year we decided we should travel and spend the summer working away. There were three of us all friends and through an agency in Lithuania we saw that there was hotel work in the Hebrides at the Dark Island Hotel, Benbecula.

It was kind of crazy we got off the ferry and a car driver stopped and said, I am a taxi – with no signs on the vehicle or anything. It was wild – narrow roads and just sheep and rocks and maybe a house or two. Anyway we arrived safely at the hotel and of course that is how it works on the Island where everybody knows everybody and where they are going.

So we worked there and enjoyed our summer there and the local folk were so nice we got on well with a local couple who looked after us – we called them Granny and Grand-dad! Then we met people from Inverness and they said we should work there. So that is how we came back for another summer this time we found work at the Inverness Airport.

We learned English at school and university but, of course, Scottish people spoke so quickly and it was quite difficult at the beginning: we just had to catch words here and there and try to make sense of it.

We were working on the catering side at the airport and it was hard work but we found that we were really valued and respected and we made friends there. So I went back and finished university and then we thought, as we had experience of working in the Highlands we would return and that is how it was, gradually we continued working here.

I had a boyfriend at that time and he wasn`t sure about moving abroad so I said: Oh, you have to visit Scotland so he came over, and we are still here and we are still together! So by the end of 2007 and into 2008 we were working and resident in Inverness. We have now got married (2011) and have a daughter of two and a half years. I work part-time now and look after our daughter.

I had worked at various jobs and I started with Highland Home Carers on a relief basis. I had studied Social Pedagogy at University so my studies were relevant to my work for example with people with learning difficulties. My husband also applied with Highland Home Carers and he got a job.

It has been a positive experience for us really, but of course we miss our parents, particularly now with our wee girl, and our parents miss her as well. But we go and travel back to Lithuania every year or so. When we travel over there we say we are going back home and when we return to Scotland we say we are going home as well!

It is really nice to have my best friends from university here in Scotland to meet up with. In fact my sister has come over to Scotland as well and she and her husband live in Aberdeen. It feels like home now in Scotland. I appreciate being valued at work – this is so important when you are busy and doing your best.

I really enjoy working here, I used to work mainly as a support worker but now I work with a colleague producing social accounts. Now I am doing Social Audits and I love my role now.

It covers such things as reviewing the mission, values and objectives of HHC and the role of service users and partners and the difference made to their lives, and of course, looking at the wider impact that HHC has. Setting up a questionnaire and posting it out, gathering information together, working on the report – yeah it's busy. We try to encourage everyone to be involved and if they have concerns to speak out and raise them.

We are settled here – we have no plans to move. Moving back to Lithuania is not on the agenda – but never say never. The move has worked for us, but I have friends who it didn`t work out for, they were maybe so homesick or could not adapt or had negative experiences and stuff. You have to be ready to take any job and maybe nowadays it is even more difficult to find a job. I am studying as well with the Open University and I am doing a Social Work degree.

I think anyone who wishes to move to another country has to respect the different culture. You have to try and learn and improve your English and try and communicate and learn new things and of course obey the laws. But we speak Lithuanian at home so our daughter will grow up with English and Lithuanian.

Djamel Baa'li – Algeria

I was born in Constantine in Algeria in 1958. My family left Algeria when I was eleven in 1969 and we went to France. My parents have French citizenship and as Algerians we have the right to move and settle in France. It used to be automatic that Algerians would get citizenship in France, but things have changed.

I went back and forth between the two countries for several years. You know the Mediterranean coast of Algeria is so beautiful, but in 1992 there was a coup which led to resistance and a Civil War which lasted throughout the 'Nineties. In those years there were bodies everywhere and terrorism on all sides. During those years it wasn`t safe at all. People had to escape to try to save themselves – just like we see in Syria today.

In 1999 Abdelaziz Bouteflika became President with the support of the military and he is still in power. There are many groups and factions operating against the regime. Algeria is a huge country probably bigger than the whole of Portugal, Spain and France together. It is a beautiful country it has everything but…

I finally left Algeria in 1993 and moved to Malta working there and then in Italy and France. In those days it was not safe to return to Algeria. Nowadays I travel to France or Tunisia and I can meet family there.

I met my wife who is from Scotland in Malta and we were married there in 1999. I had already applied to migrate to Canada and I passed the interviews and was accepted and got my visa. My wife had our first child back in Scotland and after some weeks they joined me in Quebec. It was difficult for my wife at first, she does not speak French and of course the cold is severe. I enjoyed working as an interpreter with a multi–ethnic centre and a travel agency; we had refugees from all over the Arab world and from Mexico and Columbia.

I speak Arabic, French, Italian, Spanish and a bit of Maltese so I was busy as an interpreter.

So we were settled there but after 9/11 (2001) it was very difficult for Arab people, it was like a campaign against Muslims. I was visited by the equivalent of CIA in Canada. They came to our home they accused me of working with "suspicious people" – and these were just poor refugees. They wanted me to work for them, cash in hand. I told them my religion would not allow me to visit the mosques and spy on my own people; they tried putting pressure on me taking me out in a car with a camera on me. We decided we had to do something, that was what pushed us to leave and we left in 2002.

We sold everything secretly and bought tickets one way; we had to do this in secret. We arrived finally in Glasgow via Holland I remember it was in April. It was a lovely hot day and we moved in with my parents-in-law in Inverness.

I had to apply for a visa and have a bank account with £3,500 in savings. It wasn`t easy but we had the money and we managed. My wife had applied for a house so after one month we were able to move to a flat in Dalneigh. I started working night shift in Tesco's.

We are about 16 years here in the Highlands as a family and I have met the nicest people I have ever met, I never had a problem. One obvious difference here is that if you see a policeman he gives you a smile. In my country – well it is different.

I say "my country" but you know – where I live it is my country. I have been all over and we have a saying in Arabic: *"Where I eat my bread – that is my country"*.

I have never had any racism or prejudice in Scotland. Now my wife is working as a hairdresser and I work in Morrison's and we have met a lot of good people. We have three children, all born in Inverness. They are all in Culloden Academy and they are Scottish!

I myself feel local but of course you always have Algeria in your heart, but I lost everything there, Scotland has given me so much.

I remember when I only had a travel document from Canada and a relative died suddenly in France, I had to attend the funeral. Well I went to Charles Kennedy and he helped me so much, he went to the Parliament and obtained a three-year passport for me. I obtained a full British passport in 2009.

The Highlands is my favourite place really, because it is cold, with clear, clean, fresh air. Now where I live I can look out and see the snow on Ben Wyvis.

Many of the migrants I have met are just here to earn money but they need to live here in their heads and in their hearts.

You move here to live a better life; you need to live that better life. You can do that in this country and maybe one day Scotland will become an independent country – *insha'Allah.*

Ian Westacott – Australia

I was born in 1956 in rural Australia; in Victoria about three hours' drive to the north of Melbourne. I lived in a little village with a population of around 2800.

Tobacco was the big cash crop and so it was like a "gold rush" town – people were attracted in and there was a lot of money about. The movies were on every night and many of the kids would get a sports car when they turned 18. Australia is the "land of opportunity" but that was a bit exceptional, it was sensational and funny growing up in that world.

I have recently found out that I was born in the old town hospital which was right beside the meeting place of all the aboriginals in that district. There was a huge tree there and I was fascinated by that giant tree – I always have been. That is kind of a magical strange thing, of course now I am doing a lot of work about trees. Looking back I see my childhood a lot like a paradise, living and discovering things in this amazing place. I dreamed of nothing else but this beautiful clear river and we would swim in it all the time and the magical world of mountains nearby – pure places. As kids we used to think when we would hike and things – no- one had ever walked on this ground.

But this is a kind of white man`s ignorance!

So later on I leave all this and go off to study in Melbourne and that is all about art and the pursuit of my interest in the arts. That evolved into the view that the Western world is where I had to see all that art, and that's why I travelled.

I set off travelling when I was twenty. Most Australians are encouraged to "see the world". I did a quick trip all over Europe into England and up to York where I got stuck in the snow!

So I returned to study at Melbourne to become a teacher. I taught for five years, and I decided to go back to college again and get a graduate diploma in print-making. This was a two-year course and I was successful in winning a six-month travel/work scholarship. In Aberdeen I worked at Peacock Printmakers, because the Scottish printmaking workshops have achieved some fame. I was also artistin-residence in Aberdeen and I had a show also in Edinburgh. I also worked in Paris and down in England.

But then after six months I went back to Australia. But I was very unhappy there and I had all sorts of troubles. I decided to get away and concentrate on my art work. I travelled again and met up with Sue who I had worked beside at Peacock Printmakers and we got on famously well.

Courtesy of Keith Price

In 1991 we decided to set up house together and that is how we came to live here just outside Dornoch. The regulations for residency in UK were that there was a set time that you were allowed to stay, six months. So I set off and travelled and then came back for another six months' visa permit– it was kind of bizarre and complicated. I had to go back to Australia, I decided what is it going to be life with Sue in Scotland or... it had to be Sue so I upped sticks – everything, job finished everything

"No right to work" – at a certain time I had to leave unless I got married. Even though I am an Australian and we were once part of the Colonies, I thought it was almost "just walk in there mate" – sort of thing! But I just got a stamp on my passport which gives me "right to remain", I am not allowed to go out of the country for more than two years or three I am not sure, anyway if I did I would have to get a visa and go through the whole thing again. At least my two children have dual nationality.

Moving on a permanent basis to the Highlands was an amazing

challenge for me. I grew up in a beautiful hot summer and the winters they passed fairly well. I remember the first thing I did when we moved here was to build that shed – to give us some shelter from the constant wind. I built things I learned how to drystone-dyke and renovated the house. I was young, energetic and healthy but I wasn`t allowed to work – so I relied entirely on Sue as the breadwinner.

I looked around and got some days' supply teaching jobs way over on the remoter west coast. Finally I managed to gain employment which I still have as the visiting teacher to all the primary schools; it suited me well.

You know I have struggled all the time with how do I deal with these long winters and the fact that your money doesn`t go as far as in Australia.

I always had the sense that in the summer in Australia you didn`t have to buy anything – you could grow it all – vegetables, fruit.

When our children were young we didn't go back to Australia for four

years but gee that was the hardest stretch! Anyway all my family were over there parents two brothers and a sister. I missed them terribly. My mother passed away but the rest of the family still live in Myrtle Ford in a place called Happy Valley! But with our growing family life was good.

All the same, you know, I used to dream about the gum tree because the fragrance of the eucalyptus just permeates the atmosphere so much. We lived our lives when we were young with bare feet and no shirt all summer, life was uncomplicated. There was sport of course – cricket, swimming, basketball and I came here and there was soccer and that was it.

Even now, you know, I am not completely part of the main make-up of the village here. If even today I am part of a discussion in the staff room I will hear reference to family names and family history that I have no idea about. Of course I am outside the world of the locals, I am not too worried about that but there is a gap there .

In Dornoch, well that is quite a rare world – there is obviously wealth there but a large proportion of the population is older or retired, many folk from the South have retired here. A lot of the old houses are owned by people who aren't in them because they are used as holiday homes. And there is another section of Dornoch which is the workers and they live out up the hill a bit – in a funny way.

There is a sort of cultural – I don`t know – I have Aussie mates coming to visit Britain and they say, and they probably say it quietly: "It's a bit mean here." And when they say mean – they are thinking that life here is harsher about social issues and there is a class divide, you know Australians just loathe that as a concept. There is a tall poppy syndrome in Australia – and if you stick your head up too much, if you have too much to say – you arc going to get it. Of course that is a bit unfair – but it is a different world in that respect.

If we consider ownership of huge tracts of land – well that would not happen in Australia. But maybe one of the reasons the recent election went the way it did is because people generally don't think it is fair.

It has taken me a few years to know – to actually know what people are saying! In the Highlands here there is a way of speaking that suggests meaning beyond the actual words – well I get that now but it took me a while.

I think I am accepted now in society- I am an Aussie and they know I am no threat, after all the Scots half–populated all of Australia. You know over the years I hear people say " Oh I could have gone; I could have been one of those £10 Poms". They felt they missed a huge opportunity.

Over the last year or so I have decided that here – Scotland is home, because I have finally realised that life is about the people you are with, it is not about the land that you stand on it is about what makes your life rich and worthwhile and purposeful.

I think that Scotland has benefited by immigration and I think that people feel enriched by culturally mixing.

I hope that people in Scotland are more open to different cultures I think they are – there doesn`t seem to be the fear and suspicion you can find elsewhere.

Obviously you cannot have a million people land on your doorstep but even economically you cannot survive without immigrants.

Harry Mossco Ugheli – Nigeria

I was born in Nigeria in 1979. I left Nigeria in 2004 with my brothers and sister because my father realised it was not safe for our family anymore. My father was working in Saudi Arabia in the oil industry and was, like many, a target for kidnapping. He had the opportunity to get visas for his family to travel and we children all left together in 2004. My mother is still in Nigeria.

My parents are from the same state in Nigeria but spoke different local languages – so we spoke English at home. I cannot speak my family language.

Just before we left, our house was looted and we all felt threatened. This was people who were looking to kidnap children or other family members for ransom. It just wasn`t safe to live there anymore. Many people fled the country at that time; those that were capable of taking their kids abroad did so.

We arrived in London and I met up with my father`s friends - that was the Nigerian community. But I wanted something different. I had an uncle in Scotland, in Dundee so I went there and as soon as I arrived I fell in love with the country. I knew I was in Europe then rather than an exiled Nigerian community.

But of course I missed Africa and I was lonely; when my uncle would go to work, I would go into town and I knew nobody. I spent three months with him before I moved to Edinburgh. I got an offer of a Care job in Edinburgh through a friend and I took that.

The way of life here is different but you just have to adjust. My friend and I were members of a church and we got to know a lot of people through the congregation so it was easier to settle in to this new country. I carried on living in Edinburgh for another two years and in 2007 I moved to Ireland. I lived in Dundalk close to Dublin.

I met my wife in Ireland she is from Gabon, but we are both Irish now! We only moved back to Scotland and the Highlands in January 2015; we both love Inverness and this is our home now. My sister has settled in Glasgow. I felt welcomed here and certainly I never had any problems with my work colleagues. I don't feel an outsider, it helped maybe applying for Irish nationality.

At that time a new law had come out once you have lived in Ireland for five years you can apply for naturalisation. Of course you need to be working and contributing and not have broken the law or have a criminal record. You are normally granted citizenship if you qualify. The main thing I miss about Nigeria is the weather! I can get the same food here – there is an African shop in town. My mother visits Scotland every year, and I  visited Nigeria last year but we did not spend time at home, it is not really safe there.

We have four children: a 12-year-old and a six-year-old and twins, two years old. They were all born in Ireland and they have an Irish accent! But they are learning French from my wife who had to learn English as she came from French-speaking Gabon. We also want the children to learn Scots Gaelic here in the Highlands. They will have an opportunity to speak English and Gaelic.

This is home now. If I have any problems of racism or attitudes I just blank it out. You have to keep positive and ignore it.

I have been working, paying tax and contributing in both Ireland and Scotland. I had a computer shop in Ireland at the same time as working in Care so I was very busy. At first the shop was OK but then after five years the recession came along so I closed the business.

My advice to any other migrants moving in – is to keep focused. Avoid the "fast lane" doing dodgy stuff and all that. Abide by the laws of the country, find a job and make good friends. You need to work towards "residency" though without resident status it is difficult. I used to know folk in Edinburgh who got involved in drugs and dealing as an "easy" way to make money. Well they got caught and were deported – back in Africa now struggling.

Meilo So – Hong Kong China

I was born in Hong Kong in 1963. I went to school there but at age of 14 I went to a boarding school at Abingdon near Oxford. I was four years at the boarding school and then I did a one-year Art foundation Course in College in Oxford and then three years of Art education at Brighton. Brighton was famous for graphic arts and I wanted to do illustration. I met Ron my future husband there who would later come and live in Hong Kong.

I was offered work after these courses here in UK, but as I had only a student visa, Immigration said I had to return to Hong Kong. It took a while to get established and of course art studies are not so prevalent or well regarded as civil engineering or accountancy in China.

You know my boarding school experience taught me to live on very little and that is what I did on my return to Hong Kong. As a freelance illustrator I could get an odd job and that would pay the rent for the month and so on. Of course this is hard for my parents who had spent money on my education in the west – and there was no rosy job waiting for me.

I was living in Hong Kong again for 10 years, since the Tienanmen event in 1989. My father was keen to leave as he taught Chinese history in Hong Kong Chinese University and he was worried with the hand-back to China of Hong Kong (in 1997) that there would be restrictions on his work and general freedom of expression. So he needed to leave.

Ron and I married in 1994 and we both felt that the future was too uncertain in Hong Kong so we moved back to Britain in 1996. My parents had moved to Macau and then later they went to the US where my brother was working in New Jersey and they are still there.

I hardly go back to Hong Kong now as I have no family living there.

When I look back it is interesting, I think British rule actually helped people to respect their Chinese culture and traditions. There was support for old festivals and holidays and more human-type activities.

The recent Chinese rule has little time for the old shops and trades; it is all about commerce. The old dumpling shops that were popular in various neighbourhoods have been sold through the rise of estate agents, but those friendly shops helped to make the place feel good.

I remember as a child, new shopping malls appearing and you think, oh good – air conditioning! But the whole city is just shopping malls now. Of course it is the same all over, but there is nothing you can afford because it is all chain stores and designer clothes. It is no place for ordinary people. So we moved back to Britain and settled in Worthing and lived there for seven years or so. As freelance artists we just earn enough to live with a little bit of saving. It is amazing for me in Britain you seem to do quite well but you never have any spare money!

Our daughter was born in Worthing and we liked Worthing but I was really troubled by unfriendly neighbours. They made my life so miserable and with our child becoming a toddler we lived upstairs and the neighbour downstairs – I just thought I can`t face it anymore.

My husband Ron had a childhood friend in Shetland and he went on a visit to renew this friendship. He wrote to me and said this place is friendly and musical but you might not like it as the nearest café is four miles away!

But I was keen to live in the middle of nowhere – I remember

Ron would put books on top of the piano lid so we would not be tempted to play the piano in case we got complaints.

We have a house now in the middle of nowhere – and it is away from that mad woman!

We moved to Shetland in 2002. I am not a country person – I walk on pavements. I don't know what bird is what. My life has been around cafés and restaurants – but not now. It would be hard for me to persuade a Chinese friend from Lerwick to come up here for a day.

In my experience the move has been a good one – Shetland people make you feel very important straight away they know about you and they call you by name. I never had any racist comments. Not even in the town of Lerwick, sometimes I even forget I am Chinese!

In a country district they are happy if you can contribute something to the community: for instance I play the organ and I was asked to play at a harvest festival. Since then I have played on occasions at a funeral or a wedding. It is good to belong and to contribute to the place.

Sometimes it is difficult to keep things going in a small place but I have started a choir which meets now and again. I can have a great time making music with people and we don't have to speak, we can play music for an hour or so communicating, but not speaking!

I think you have to be strong enough in yourself to live in a place with long, dark winters and with isolation. Sometimes there are down moments and I take a supplement called Fucodian. It is a seaweed product and it strengthens your mood and I feel able to cope. You see I don't smoke and I don't drink, but this works for me.

It is not anonymous here we all rely on each other, you must speak out when something is wrong – but you can feel a bit paranoid about that.

I feel at home here and I like the people but most folk will not ask about my background. Sometimes I will feel more comfortable with other outsiders I think it is because we share the same feeling of trying to fit in. I have a very good German friend who I trust and can speak about everything.

I am a British citizen but I don't feel specifically British or Chinese I am just a person.

My father was born in South China by accident but he is really a Hakka which means "guest people" and in earlier times they maybe walked all the way from Siberia. Hakka move around and they do not have a traditional home. So I am a Hakka and I move. My father for example – anywhere he is, he is happy.

We will stay here; we moved here to a great extent to bring up our daughter here but in the future if she moves away permanently things may change...

For those moving in to a new place Shakespeare has some advice, from "*Much Ado about Nothing*": "Love many, trust few – do wrong to none."

Trust few – this means don't give yourself away, because you are fragile migrating to a new country. A foreigner can feel unprotected but we learn how to look out for ourselves.

Gleny Tomalin (née Baca Tapia) – Peru

I was born in Cusco Peru in 1966. I went to a Catholic primary school in Cusco managed by Nuns, and I went to do my secondary education in Lima. I lived with my aunty there, my father`s sister. When I began my nursing degree I returned to Cusco. I wanted to be a doctor but I couldn`t get a place; there were only 18 places on that course.

We did basic nursing and then over four years we covered all the specialisms including community nursing. At that time development projects were going ahead supported by the German Technical Cooperation Agency (GTZ). With their support we opened a library. I learned a lot from this Project particularly from the emphasis on Public Health into medical curriculum and the fact that they brought experts together from all over Central, South America and Europe.

So a German Professor who published several research articles and papers on Primary Health Care and Public Health, offered me a job in research in Puerto Maldonado in the Amazon region of Peru on the Madre de Dios river, a tributary of the Amazon.

The focus was the control of Malaria – trying to implement control measures based on community participation. What we were involved in was impregnating malaria nets with Permethrin obtained from chrysanthemum flowers which acts as an insecticide and repellent that only affects the mosquito who transports the malaria parasite. It is effective and simple so it can be done locally. We worked in 22 communities and also promoted health education.

I worked there for two years and then obtained a similar public health post on the Pacific Coast of Columbia in Rio San Juan; and I worked there for 18 months.

On the Pacific Coast and in Puerto Buenaventura most of the Afro-Columbian peoples are descended from slaves but they are from different tribal groups. It was difficult to involve and win participation in our health programmes. They worked extracting timber. They live with very basic facilities no treated water, sewage works or electricity.

I lived in Cali, Columbia for five years nursing in a variety of health areas. Nurses have some status there and were referred to as "Jefes" (bosses). I worked in a clinic run by nuns, with support and advice from medical consultants – good pay and good conditions. They routinely performed operations and I worked in Intensive  care. During this time I was studying Family Health Specialism at the University of Cali. I also worked in Public Health and I became a clinical instructor for auxiliary nurses for a year before I went to Africa. I loved Cali in Columbia – it is always spring there and people are very happy there!

I was thinking to do more in the sense of really assisting people in need. So I sent my CV to a Development Agency in Los Angeles. I heard back that I would be offered a year's work contract in Angola.

There I worked with the rebel forces which had been supported by Cuban and Italian and French solidarity brigades.

I nursed there for two years and as a bonus I met my husband Phil who was working with Concern Worldwide. Anyway Phil was thinking of returning to UK – he grew up in Yorkshire. When we came to settle in the UK, we went to live in West Sussex, Phil went to study Environment, Development and Policy at Sussex University.

When we arrived in Sussex I registered with the Nursing and Midwifery Council (NMC) to be able to work and I had to do six months placement in a local hospital. Afterwards I started to work as a trained nurse. After five years we saw an advert for a job in the Highlands.

All we knew about the Highlands before we moved here was that there was beautiful landscape, lots of lochs and not many people!

So we moved north and Phil was appointed to the post of Area Development Manager, but soon this post was deleted and he became East Sutherland and Edderton Ward Manager.

So I applied initially for the Nursing Bank with NHS Highland and afterwards I had a permanent job in Lawson Memorial Hospital Golspie.

My heart is always on the community health side and I am now working as a Community Nurse in East Sutherland. I provide care to older adults; our main focus is to allow them to maintain independence and prevent hospital admission if possible. We also support people with chronic conditions, palliative care and end-of-life care, through applying holistic assessment and patient-centred management.

I love this Community Participation side of my work, but there is a lot of work to do. Even encouraging a change in attitude takes time; people can be assisted to take more control over their health and care – to be more autonomous.

I might do this by listening and motivating people to see that through small changes in their routine they can enjoy a better quality of life: simple exercises – skin care, managing weight, diet and nutrition and exercise. Really it is straightforward if people could be encouraged away from processed foods high in sugar and salt content, but low in nutrition.

Also people could take more responsibility instead of relying on pills. Some older people are dependent on health care workers. They could be assisted to take more control.

But of course we need to change the Health Care system as well. No matter the age of our patients simple interventions can improve the quality of life. I raise these issues with my colleagues and with relatives of older patients. We are having some success. We have a good team of nurses who wish to empower their patients. And of course we receive regular in-house training in different aspects of health and health behaviour change.

As a family we are happy; here in Dornoch people are accepting of you, maybe compared to the South of England, where I felt more anonymous.

I never met one Latin American in the South but when I arrived here the minister's wife was from Peru!

When I meet new people they ask where I am from – always they will know someone who has a link with Peru or South America. I feel at home here – as long as I can work and my family are happy.

Difficulties – initially I applied for different jobs and the feedback referred to me as a poor communicator. I have never had a problem understanding Highlanders – they generally speak clearly. I have two boys at secondary school, and I had a lot of support from other parents, here I feel very much part of the community.

I see myself as British but I have dual nationality. It is too long a process achieving citizenship, too much paperwork.

You know the empty landscape here reminds me of Peru. I try to visit Peru at least every five years and my mother has visited here.

People who are moving to the Highlands should really try to integrate into the local community. The next generation will integrate maybe better than us, but we all need the opportunity to work and to contribute.

In Spanish we have a saying which means wherever you go – do what you see. *"Donde vayas haz lo que vieras"*.

Petra and Arafeh Alashi – Czech Republic and Palestine

(Also their lovely daughters; Mariam and Nina)

Arafeh Alashi was born in Amman, Jordan on 22nd January 1968 Petra Alashi was born in Jilemnice Czechoslovakia on 30th October 1981

Alashi`s Story: I was born and brought up in Amman because my family were forced out of Palestine and settled in Jordan.

My family originally came from Arammla which is near Haifa, and even today part of my family live in Palestine and part in Jordan.

It is very hard; when I was in Jordan I felt Palestinian but when I was in Palestine I felt Jordanian.

I didn`t feel comfortable with both countries – maybe this is one of the reasons that led me out of the whole region to try to find my identity who am I; where did I come from, and I am very very pleased that I came to Scotland. I chose Scotland because there is a similarity in a way…

Petra`s story: In 2008 I came to Scotland to improve my English as part of my studies, and I decided to extend my stay. I was studying teacher training in the Czech Republic. My professor agreed to keep my place at College/Uni open for me, but I went back for a visit and explained I would be staying on.

I had a job at the Mustard Seed restaurant in Inverness and I got on well there and became second chef in charge of the sweets and desserts. My sister who was here helped me find this job and she spoke on my behalf. I stayed on at the Mustard Seed for just over three years. I also attended the college and took a course to improve my English and enrolled on a child development course which I am still studying.

I found life in the Highlands completely different but I liked it here and the people I met. I was hoping to settle but speaking English was hard – oh people spoke so fast! I didn`t even know what people were saying to me at first. I didn`t even know how to ask for coffee or anything – I was so quiet.

Arafeh: When I was living in Jordan I had an opportunity to work for a British company as a tour guide – I was their representative in Amman. I worked for this company for two years and then I was invited to Britain in 1990 to continue working with them – with my interest in History and Geography I was leading private and group tours.

After a while I decided to start my own company offering tours I started this in Manchester and I called it CCH travel. I would lead tours all over Europe and the Middle East I did that for almost 13 years, for much of that time I was based in Cyprus. During travels with groups I had visited Scotland and every time I came up to Scotland I thought there was something about it… I don't know what, but I found the people friendly and more accepting of outsiders. That was my experience anyway and I thought it would be easier for me to settle down in Scotland.

So it was the friendliness of the people and the scenery and somehow I felt kind of connected in a way as a Palestinian I could understand a people who had also migrated maybe through persecution or economic necessity.

So I thought, with my travel company my home could be anywhere, and in 1998 I decided to make my home in Scotland so I travelled north and found a house in Tong in Lewis just north of Stornoway. I thought this is an adventure! I wanted to live with the islanders and I did and I loved it and I stayed for three and a half years. I was still able to travel and meet up with visitors and take them round Europe and the Middle East.

My neighbours in Tong were Gaelic-speaking and I got on really well with them. I remember when I was moving in and I had been away, when I arrived home it was late and I was really hungry – there was a casserole waiting for me. My neighbour had made this lovely casserole for me – oh I enjoyed it! This was hospitality, as I remember. It said to me – you are welcome.

My lovely neighbour, her name was Cathy – she is dead now – God rest her soul, she visited me once and said I would like to tell you about the Island. She said: Here we are quite religious – would you mind not hanging your washing out on a Sunday or doing things – working outside on a Sunday. I respected that and even though the only dry day might be a Sunday I never put washing out and I had no problems whatsoever.

In those days there was no ferry service and the only bus took the congregation to church. For me if you wish to be accepted and respected in a country you need to respect and accept their laws their traditions and their culture.

If people have a fear of the unknown they keep to themselves and keep their traditions and culture to themselves. Then others may say: why do you do this – who are you – where did you come from – then they may get worried and keep their distance. But if you are happy to mix and explain your background where you come from and your traditions well, they get to know all of that and all this fear or suspiciousness will disappear. In this way I have managed for over 20 years in Scotland – I have never had a problem.

Petra: For me one of the things that makes me feel at home and reminds me of home is the landscape and natural environment of the Highlands. I am from the countryside in the Czech Republic and there are mountains, lochs and green valleys.

The people here I have found friendly and helpful. We have

made lovely friends here and they have helped so much to make us feel at home. When I was in hospital and unsure where to go - right away a nurse asked me are you okay, do you need help? Generally people seem to look out for you and will approach to ask if you need help. I was surprised by this – but it was and is a nice feeling.

Arafeh: We now run a Bed and Breakfast business in Inverness and it is through this business that Petra and I met.

Petra is Catholic and I am Muslim but we will encourage our daughters to learn about Scotland and religion so that when they are older they can decide on their own beliefs, if they wish to follow our traditions, Islam or Christianity or not, that is up to them.

We spoke about the children's future education in Inverness.

We have approached the local school which is close and it is a very good school but they do not offer education in Gaelic the traditional language of Scotland. They do offer Polish and I can see why, but I would like my children to learn and speak Gaelic which is unique to Scotland.

I would like my daughters to be proud of their Scottish roots, they were born here and if they knew the language of Scotland, they would know where they are from. Their mother is from Czech Republic and their father Palestine but they will be Scottish so in the future when people ask what is Scotland to you they will be able to say Scotland is my home.

As parents we will do our best to give our children these strong Scottish cultural roots. We feel this country offers every opportunity to make something of yourself. Despite our accent this is our home!

Father Piotr Rytel – Poland

Courtesy of Inverness Courier

I was born in Wysokie Mazowieckie, in north-east Poland on the 25th July 1980.

I went through my primary school and secondary school in Wysokie Mazowieckie and then I studied at the Seminary. I finished my studies at the seminary in 2005. I then obtained work as a Parish Assistant and worked in country areas of Poland for eight years.

I enjoyed my time there but I had in my heart the growing feeling that I must go somewhere, but I did not know where and when yet!

But I remember a Parish meeting with fellow priests when I heard that there might be an opportunity to work with the Polish community in Scotland. I thought that this would be for me so I first I went to Aberdeen. I worked with Bishop Hugh Gilbert in the Diocese of Aberdeen, I stayed there for around six months and then I returned to Poland, but I had a plan to return and at the end of August 2013 I arrived in the Highlands.

I remember feeling good when I arrived in Inverness; I liked the town, not too big and it reminded me of my own region. I started here in this church as parish assistant but also as a Polish Chaplain for our people in the Highlands.

I did not find it difficult to feel settled here in the Highlands because I had already been travelling and working outside my home district in Poland. But as a priest, part of my job is to help support and encourage people and most importantly be with them, and of course that helps me feel more part of the community.

I was worrying about how I would manage with my English which was difficult to begin with – but I was using a lot of Polish and that was no problem. I was welcomed here.

I went to the college here once a week to attend English language classes and that helped.

I miss my family and friends in Poland of course but I can go back regularly – there are good connections; also my sister has visited me here. I had always played football and we had a league when I was at the Seminary so that was something else I could get involved in. I went to school with the former Celtic goalkeeper Lucas Zaluska.

Our football club FC Polonia in Inverness was founded by two Polish workers. So I joined and we have fun and can socialise together – it is a good team spirit – but you also have to play football!

I think when you are moving to a new country you have to be open to all those you meet, and if you have an opportunity to study and improve your English, take it.

It is important also to improve your work, your occupation and try to achieve Scottish equivalent qualifications which will allow you to work in your chosen field. You need to find out about health and safety regulations – we can help each other to do this.

It is hard at first for immigrants because they live closely maybe with family or one or two friends; this is a closed group but they need to open up.

I am for integration and this is good and necessary but you must save and celebrate your own culture also. We have regular parties and picnics to celebrate our Polish culture but nowadays they are open for everyone to come along and enjoy.

We often see these occasions to fundraise for a local charity.

Apart from meeting and knowing people the landscape also helps me feel at home; I have everything here – mountains, lochs and sea. All of this is near at hand.

But it is not always easy – one of my parishioners has told me that he had been accused of coming here and taking a job away from a local person. But I think if you want to work you will work and that is the same for everyone.

There are many people in Scotland, older people, who remember that first Polish emigration after the Second World War and the Poles who were working alongside them helping to build up the country. One of the days when we come together is Remembrance Day. There is a Polish war memorial in Invergordon and we have a joint service there, all of us alongside descendants of British soldiers and Polish soldiers remembering together.

Now these days we still have young people coming over especially from the poorer areas of Poland – you can understand if they have no prospect of a job. Some may stay for just a year or two but some have settled here and raised children here and of course there are some inter-marriages between Scots and Poles.

On the wider political front, things have changed in Poland, like everywhere. During the time of Solidarnos we were together against a communist system – but now, like here, political parties seem to be for themselves – their own Party and no other.

If you have a different view in this situation it is very hard to find compromise.

Religion could be – or should be a more embracing approach.

Catherine Campos Rio – Galicia, Spain

I was born in 1971 in a small village near Santiago de Compostela in Galicia, Northern Spain.

Our family moved when I was six years old to Venezuela. They could not find work in Galicia and we had a cousin in Venezuela, who had a carpentry business so my father was able to get a work contract which allowed us to emigrate. We spent almost 20 years in Venezuela, going once or twice a year to Spain for holidays.

We decided to leave around 1995 and completed the move six months before Chavez came to power. We knew what was going to happen because we had a relative who had moved to Cuba and the Castro government took all his belongings, after thirty years of hard work he had to leave Cuba.

I had been studying and training in Medicine in Venezuela and when Chavez came to power many of my friends left for the US but I was keen to return to Spain; I always had this in mind.

I went back to Galicia and enrolled in specialist medical training which was available in Barcelona. I was offered a contract in Barcelona and I worked there as a GP from the year 2000. I finished this specialist training in 2005. I was offered a post in a semi-rural area about an hour from the city of Barcelona. This post offered experience in A&E and in palliative care and I worked there for some years.

But it was not a true rural practice so I started to look for a more rural post. I was looking for a post in Galicia. However my sister had been working in Shetland and she saw this post on the Island of Yell advertised. I applied and started in 2013.

When I arrived in Shetland I thought this is just like the place I was born, near the sea in Galicia, this is like home, rain included.

The weather – well in Galicia it rains from November until May and then it stops for a while and then it really rains!

I know some people think this is "isolated" but they don`t know what isolated is. In South America where I did my early training there were only two land lines for three thousand people. In the

town where I worked it was two hours to the city but with the heavy rains the road would be impassable. We used to talk with the hospital staff by radio. I like the islands and the people have welcomed me; they are really nice and they have invited me to their houses – but I cannot acccpt. I am on call the whole time and I cannot rely on the mobile signal.

When you need to evacuate a patient out of hours it is necessary to make several phone calls to ambulance control, NHS 24, the practice nurse and the hospital. If I go off the islands maybe to Barcelona, Galicia, or even to Lerwick, I can only go at a time that is suitable for an associate GP to cover for me.

The continuous demands of out-of-hours cover in this single-handed practice has forced me to leave. My health has deteriorated, very few hours' sleep, impossible to go out for a simple walk, because as I said, you must be near to the phone and the mobile signal is not good. I will be going to Bixter next month where I will be working in a shared practice with no out-of-hours work. But in Yell there are related stresses, for example I visited a patient with chest pains and I could not get an ambulance there until two hours later.

On the neighbouring island there are two doctors to cover six hundred patients. In Yell we have one thousand patients and only one doctor on the island. I have to meet all the health demands and out-of-hours single-handed.

I rely on an excellent senior nurse on Fetlar who advises me on the health of the sixty patients there. I make regular visits there. I am concerned that the post here will not be advertised until I leave. But I want to work in Shetland and contribute to the medical services and I am interested in Community Health initiatives – but I do not have the time here on this island.

I hope to stay on in the islands – but this post being on call twenty -four hours a day, seven days a week is unmanageable, say for more than three weeks. After this you start to get very exhausted.

We are delighted to hear that Dr Campos Rio is now working with a medical practice based in Bixter on Shetland's South Mainland.

Abs Seoud – Inverness

I was born in Inverness in 1980 but when I was a year old my mother returned to Jordan. I was brought up in Amman, Jordan and I stayed there until I was 12 years old and then we moved to Aquaba on the Red Sea coast.

My mother is Scottish/Italian and she is from the Serafini family from Barga. My father is Palestinian. I must have Scottish genes because when I was growing up I felt I was the only red-haired boy in Jordan! I learned English first and then Arabic once I attended one of the old King Hussein schools in Amman.

I was not keen to stay on in Jordan after schooling because at that time your progress into a job was about who you know. Although my father had connections, I needed to get away and build my own life. Also when I looked ahead and thought about marriage and maybe raising a family that would be hard in Jordan and depend on family contacts. After the Gulf War everything in Jordan went to tatters.

In 1997/98 I went to Dubai and worked in hotels. It is a man-made place – no cultural history, in fact you hardly see local families. Not a place you would want to settle in, but the people I worked with from Britain said I maybe should go back there and study and obtain qualifications so that I could get a better position within the hotel industry.

I applied for Inverness College and got on to their HNC course but I could not afford to continue my studies so I got a job in the Co-op here in Inverness. That is where I learned my first Scottish word – tattie, because I had been asked by this lovely lady can you show me where the neeps and tatties are? She was a pensioner and she looked out for me, teaching me other words and helping me improve my Scottish accent!

I worked part-time and continued studying until 2001. I got a job then in Costa Coffee and I loved it. The people were fantastic and I met a lot of people and made friends. I could understand people, I had gone to Glasgow for a month but I struggled there understanding folk. I know my English was a mix of American and English, not so helpful in Scotland.

Once I had saved up enough money I was able to enrol in Queen Margaret University in Edinburgh to study International Hospitality, a year of study and an additional six months work placement.

I was able to return to Inverness on placement because Costa Coffee gave me the assistant manager's post. I was the youngest manager in Scotland for Costa. Once I finished my studies I decided to stay on working in Costa. I enjoyed working there and after four years I became the general manager.

I moved on to Bella Italia where I managed the place for twelve years. I liked meeting and talking to the customers and stayed till 2014.

Looking back over my time in Inverness I would say that I did struggle; at least for the first three years. After big cities like Amman and Dubai it seemed everyone knew everybody here but I was outside that and I did feel lonely and sometimes depressed. I got myself a computer so it was just me and the computer – and my friendly customers.

I suppose that is why I was happy working sixty hours and more a week. I was raised a Muslim and I am not a big drinker, and I missed Arabic food, so I thought I am not going to be able to join the culture here. I played football and went swimming and that helped.

Inverness people are great and after some time I made good friends. But my name was odd and being ginger – well maybe I felt a bit of an alien! So I shortened my name to Abs.

Through my work I was travelling to Aberdeen and Glasgow so I began to feel more Scottish. Generally I found people were kind and welcoming but there were a few occasions that people would react to my name and say what are you doing here? I tried to explain where I came from and the different cultures and what work I was doing.

Many of the older people I met had connections with Jordan through their military experience. Jordan was always linked to Britain through royal links and a lot of British army training etc. In the Jordanian army radio engineers were probably 90% British.

I went back to Jordan during my time with Bella Italia – they kept the job open for me and I was six months there but I could not settle, I felt up-rooted. I missed Inverness, why I am not sure, after all the weather can be depressing, but I feel safe in Inverness.

In Jordan it is different, my father was Palestinian and he had left Palestine for Egypt in 1948 with his father who married an Egyptian in Cairo.

But Palestinians are not given an Egyptian passport; Egypt in those days ensured that the Palestinians were kept

Abs with son Alexander

separate, no assimilation. In Jordan, King Hussein gave Palestinians temporary Jordanian passports and if you remained over a longer period you could apply for a full Jordanian Passport. My father was able to get this passport through the hospitality industry in which he had advanced.

At the end of the day as Palestinians we have few rights and even in Jordan if I was to have a fight with a Jordanian I would be the one in big trouble.

Here in Scotland if there is trouble there is a fair investigation into who caused the issue, but I think in Jordan the foreign one is regarded as guilty and asked why have you come to this country causing trouble?

I remember in Scotland I was involved in a bit of trouble at a club, not a fight but an upset and the police were called but although they knew my accent was different they just interviewed us and I was treated like a normal person I wasn`t guilty just because I was foreign. I have heard people say there is corruption in this country, but I have not seen it, it is not like Jordan. I am afraid in many Arabic countries *who* you know, still plays a big part and bribery is not uncommon. The dictatorships that we have in many Arabic countries are supported by tribes or clans who look after their own. This corrupts the politics of the country as well, you can see this in Gaza where the people are misled through loyalties into senseless attacks – they are going to lose.

So Scotland for me, given my experience is a place that is open – if you obey the law you will be protected.

As I said my name makes me visible. I am Sunni and about three years ago I got a visit from a group of Shi`ites. Now these groups are part of Islam but they are very much not part of each other. Religion in my experience has been a way to control people and here was another example. They wanted me to support and be a part of charitable efforts to support Pakistani Muslims; this was after 9/11. In Jordan many of these groups were banned as they were seen to be supporting terrorist organisations. I went to the police station and explained that I did not want to be part of any such group and it was only because of my name that I had been identified. I was very upset and I do not want these people to damage this country like they have other countries.

Although I feel Scottish and Arabian this is our home now; my wife is from Poland but we are settled in the Highlands. My son Alexander who is now four and a half was born at the same hospital that I was born in. He is now pretty fluent in English and Polish with only a little Arabic. This is the first year I am running this guest house so I can spend more time with him. My wife's family can visit here but my father cannot. He has not seen his grandson. He applied for a visa but was refused – the British embassy does not give an explanation for refusal.

If you move into a country like Britain you need to work. You need to work hard and then you can get on. I started unloading bags of tatties from the back of a lorry and worked my way up.

You can struggle for the first two or three years but after that things should open up – for me Scottish people have been amazing they are proud of their country and they are proud of their culture.

I feel proud myself saying that, my son will grow up Scottish and we as a family are much safer here.

Almas Butt – Jhelum, Punjab Province, Pakistan

I was born in Jhelum Pakistan in 1988. We later moved to Kharian to be safer. My mother, my sister and I left Pakistan in 2002 when I was 14 and we moved to the UK. My father had already been working in the UK for more than 10 years and of course we missed him and wanted to be with him. When the date for leaving finally arrived I was very excited although it was so difficult to leave all the cousins and other family members there.

So by January 2003 we were together as a family in Edinburgh. We have wider family in Manchester and London but not in Scotland. I prefer Scotland because it is less crowded. I know it is easier to be part of the immigrant community in the South, but I prefer the more integrated communities that we have in Scotland. I found that you are more in touch with your neighbours who care about you here in the North. For me if you are going to live in this country you have to be part of the society.

I work now in the University of Edinburgh and I have seen groups of students from different countries stick to their own national group it makes it difficult for them to improve their English. It is important to get out of that comfort zone.

When I arrived in Scotland I finished my schooling at Firrhill Academy Edinburgh. I had learned and used English in Pakistan so my grammar was OK but I had to work at understanding and using the local accent – there were good facilities at school and it was quite relaxed. I remember noticing the lack of respect for teachers; in Pakistan if we addressed a teacher we had to stand up and ask permission!

I had to get used to these new ways and I really missed my friends. But we were on the phone or talking on-line. I am still in touch with some of them today. So I suppose for the first two years I was living in a closed-off world and had not got the confidence to communicate, but then slowly I began to make friends here.

I have never faced racism here. I know people who have, but I don't take things personally, although I remember at the beginning at school another pupil said to me, "So do you like Osama Bin Laden?

In 5th year at school there was a lot of pressure to start thinking about university and of course my family wanted me to become a doctor. I was uncertain about what I wanted to do; I did not have good enough grades. So I missed the opportunity of doing Medicine.

So with this family pressure I started studying Biological Sciences, but by year three I realised that this was not going to get me into Medicine. There was no way. I graduated in 2011 but without industrial experience it is difficult to get a job in sciences. Anyway I got a job at Tesco and won promotion to be a supervisor I worked there for two years and then I was faced with redundancy – finished 2013.

I now work in Edinburgh University as a Senior Administration Officer in Student Services.

Some years ago in 2008 my family moved north to Inverness. My father had been working in Burton's Biscuit factory on the conveyor belts but had health problems - a heart attack and a hand injury. In our family and culture we do not claim benefits, although my father was registered disabled. So he decided he would need to go into his own business. He had been the only one of the family earning money as my two brothers and I were studying with a younger sister at school.

Things were difficult; he heard through a friend that there was a property to lease in Inverness. So he went north alone in the winter of 2008/2009.It was a tough decision because he had worked hard in Edinburgh and had a lot of friends there. Anyway he took over an empty shop unit and had to build shelves from scratch. It took him almost three months to get going but he built up a trade with many newspaper deliveries and groceries and confectionery in the shop.

Soon he was joined by my mother and sister, with the brothers going back and forth until in 2013 the whole family moved here. I worked in Inverness on a placement with Tesco but the company restructured and I got the university job down in Edinburgh. So I live during the week in Edinburgh but I am helping the family here in Inverness most weekends. I have made friends over many years in Edinburgh. I feel at home there.

In my younger years I always felt Pakistani, and I would feel people look at me as if I was a Pakistani. Over the last five years it has changed, when I am talking to people I feel myself as a "normal" Scottish person. I don't have that insecurity that I once had thinking that they might not be as friendly to me because I am a Pakistani.

People in Scotland have been so welcoming – it's unbelievable. Yes, you do get an odd few here or there, if they are drunk they might hurl abuse...

We got British citizenship through the Life in the UK Test. It asked questions that none of my Scottish friends knew the answer to, but my father and I passed it first time.

I travelled back to Pakistan in 2009; before then there was a lot of terrorism, every day there would be attacks. When you are there you realise that life continues in spite of everything.

I love what the Scottish Government has done for migrants creating a positive story and there has been a community welcome as well. I do wish though that people were more open to other sources of information rather than the traditional media which can be so negative. Sadly people seem to believe what they read in *The Sun* or *The Daily Mail*. There is so much misinformation going around – so many agendas – you need to do your own research.

I can see why people look at Muslims that they know, such as the local shopkeepers or friends from work or college and they do not want to believe that this person wants to harm them in any way.

But then there is the media and TV talking about violence and terrorism. So they end up questioning themselves – should we believe the media or our own instincts? That is a tricky situation to be in and I don't blame them for it. I think also that the Muslim community needs to do more. I attend the Central Mosque in Edinburgh. I go there especially on Fridays and on week days there are conducted tours for school groups and Arabic classes. I love that open-ness, the Mosque is a place of worship but beyond that it needs to be an education centre and a community hub. Work needs to be done definitely on the Muslim community`s part.

I remember a few years ago during heavy snowfall the Mosque organised a squad with shovels and we cleared people`s driveways. They really appreciated it and offered us tea or coffee – that is what brings communities together.

We cannot isolate ourselves; any new migrants should mix with people and trust their neighbours. The worst thing to do is to stick only to your own community – that is not going to help you or your own ethnic community.

New people when they arrive here need to remember that they need to act responsibly; they will be seen as a representative of that culture. Whatever they do they will be judged and there may be a backlash against their family or wider community.

Yousra Martin – Salt, Jordan

(with Helen Farrelly – British Sign Language (BSL)/English Interpreter)

I was born in the agricultural town of Salt, Jordan in 1965. I left Jordan to come to study in Doncaster for two years, where I met my husband who is from Scotland. We went back to Jordan for four years and then moved to the Highlands – Inverness.

Oh it was hard, I missed my family and I was so homesick. As I am deaf I had to learn a new sign language. I already could sign in Arabic but I had to learn British Sign Language (BSL). It was difficult but after some time I could communicate through BSL. I now teach BSL to others. There are regional variations in BSL so some of the signs I use in the Highlands are different to the signs I picked up in the early days in Doncaster.

I was born deaf and have developed Usher Syndrome which is genetic and causes visual impairment - it kept me isolated. When I think back on my early experience I was unhappy and ready to go back. My husband was working and I was alone at home. I was lonely and I was even anxious about leaving the house; that went on for about four years, so I couldn`t make friends.

It took a while to get over this but really it was thanks to Alison Pyott of the Workers Educational Association who visited me and invited me to join a course. The people I got to know were so friendly and kindly, it is this really that has helped me begin to feel settled here in the Highlands.

I have been teaching sign language here in Inverness for eight years. It is always enjoyable meeting the BSL students and I find teaching them to sign is rewarding.

I feel much more confident now and I am sure it is thanks to the groups I am involved in and the people I have met. Nowadays I will make the first move and contact people to make friends or to see if they need help. I never hold back!

At times I have gone in to schools on a voluntary basis and talked to them about my homeland, deafness and sign language. I have three children: aged 17, 15 and 11 years and they are happy at school.

We are settled as a family here in the Highlands but I still miss the life in Jordan. We go back for a visit now and again. I have a lot of family there and of course I miss them.

I think it will be hard for anyone settling in a new country. They need to meet people and make friends and maybe join a group.

I am part of the group: Highland Multicultural Friends. I was invited to join by Alison who is so kind-hearted – it has helped me so much.

(This group, some of whom are pictured above with Yousra, has been going for ten years now and aims to help people avoid social isolation, runs a cooking club, a sewing group and children's activities, all in a bid to encourage friendships and smooth integration into society.)

I am sorry to say you would not find this group support and such organisations in Jordan. In the past, I have benefited also from support from social work services, sadly in Jordan there is no help of that kind. The only help people can get is through their own family. With the political situation there and the continuing wars it does not look like it will improve in the near future. It is not safe now with more refugees they have heightened security measures, it is very tense. Even when we attended my brother's wedding recently the police arrived and examined papers. I kept very quiet and respectful – it is the only way.

Fazlu Miah – Bangladesh

I was born in 1957 in a village of over 1000 people in Bangladesh.

My father was already working in London and we moved to join him in 1971. I moved to Sussex for work in 1982 and then up to Inverness in 1987. I had a friend working here and he asked me up to join him in business that was an Indian restaurant in Ness Walk.

After three years I moved to work in the Rajah Restaurant I am still working there. I have four children who have graduated now and they are working away in Edinburgh and Glasgow, they may come back. They feel very much Scottish.

I always felt very welcome here in the Highlands, I never felt unwanted. You always miss your own country but I have family here in London and now in Scotland.

In Bangladesh of course in the village we had a very close connection with everyone. In London you know nothing, it is a different world! But I had learned English in Bangladesh; there we spoke Bengali with English as a second language.

So I was over 10 years in London and I believe it was a very good move to Inverness. Inverness seemed to be very small in 1987; it has grown now of course. My wife and I feel at home here. The community helps each other and now that we have our Mosque here we can worship together and develop our community work.

Although I have everything here, because my childhood was spent in a village in Bangladesh,that feels close to me – it is part of me. That is the part I miss.

Even though the new country is healthier or has a better standard of living you are still drawn to your early experience. You cannot block these experiences from your body and mind. I have re-visited Bangladesh maybe four times over the years.

So I have really three connections Bangladesh, London and Inverness – and they all pull me.

My father was working with the British Merchant Service

serving on a ship; that is how he came to Britain. So I now have my own British citizenship.

The restaurant trade is very busy but you meet people and it is easier when you are working. In Inverness it was easy to get to know people and feel part of the community. With my children attending Crown Primary and Millburn Academy I met with teachers and they were always trying to help and support my children`s progress.

I felt the local people liked me, I have never felt alone here. I have nothing but praise for the education system and health services, also law and order – I feel a lot safer. I feel at home, you know, I feel if I go anywhere in Scotland I will probably meet someone I know!

Sometimes you think it would be good to live again in Bangladesh but I know I would feel a migrant there, two generations have grown up since I left I wouldn't know so many people – everything has changed.

I remember in a certain area of Bangladesh where there were many British people working in transport and the military there was clothing designed based on tartan so maybe that is a Scottish connection. I am reminded of Bangladesh when I see the natural environment here in the Highlands plants, trees and the empty lands. I used to drive to Loch Ness and enjoy nature.

Learning the language is the first thing new arrivals have to do. Have a good relation with local people; see them as human beings. You need to see the big picture which means that human relationships are about give and take. You learn how to live with people how to share things. Through this sharing and helping each other we become one human family.

You know we have to love each other – otherwise there is no solution.

Acknowledgements...

I am grateful and indebted to so many people who have helped to bring this idea to fruition.

A big thankyou and a salute to all those who pointed me in the right direction; made introductions and suggested contacts:

Martin Pieraccini; Lawrence Jamieson; Stephen Pennington; Anna MacGillivray; Hilary Lawson; Carol Gunn; Sue Jane Taylor; Anne Sutherland; Arafeh Alashi; Imam Vali Hussein; Dr Waheed Khan.

Many thanks to good friends Mike McDonnell and Ian Kerr; as always their advice support and critical analysis has been invaluable, and my old friend Bette McArdle who generously brought her professional skills to sub-editing and preparation for publication.

I benefited so much from the encouragement and guidance from various organisations and groups: Highland Home Carers; Inverness Masjid; Highland Multicultural Friends, and signer Helen Farrelly; Migrant Voice; Highland Council's Equality Officer – Rosemary MacKinnon; University of the Highlands and Islands History Department particularly Elizabeth Ritchie, David Worthington and Ian Robertson.

Many thanks to the team at The Print Shop, Merkinch.

There are two people who were crucial to the success of this venture. Jim Hunter, apart from his more visible talents, is so generous with his skills and experience. His enthusiasm for this project enabled me to develop it further and re-ignited my own commitment.

And my wife Irene: she is not only completely supportive but her organisational ability and innate good sense keep me on the right track.

Thank you to all.

R.B. MacLeod
Skerray, 2016